Beyond the Pale

Copyright © 2012 by Jeffrey A. Herring

First Printing

All rights reserved. No part of this book may be reproduced in any manner whatsoever without written permission from the publisher, except in the case of brief quotations embodied in critical articles and reviews. For information email Jeffrey A. Herring @ mr.h3rring@gmail.com.

Credits
Cover art designed by Jacob Herring

All scripture quotations, unless otherwise stipulated, are taken from *The Message*. Copyright © 1993, 1994, 1995, 1996, 2000, 2001, 2002. Used by permission of NavPress Publishing Group.

ISBN 978-0-9884673-0-9

Dedication

To Kelly, Kourtney, Maggi, and Jack - without whom this journey would be less vibrant, joyous, and important.

And to my friends, in all of their varied shapes, sizes, and flavors – you are Jesus to me.

TABLE OF CONTENTS

Author's Note i
Chapter 1 - Beyond the Pale 1
Chapter 2 - Them and Us 5
Chapter 3 - Juxtaposed Jesus 11
Chapter 4 - Battling Bias 17
Chapter 5 - Tolerance 23
Chapter 6 - Organism vs. Organization 29
Chapter 7 - Rebel in Sandals 35
Chapter 8 - Baby Jesuses 43
Chapter 9 - R.E.S.P.E.C.T. 49
Chapter 10 - Practically Related 57

AUTHOR'S NOTE

Before you consider reading this book, I have a confession to make. Actually, I have a couple of confessions to make...

My first admission is that this isn't a book written for public consumption, at least not initially. I'm someone who uses writing as a means of catharsis, a way to process what is going on in my life and mind. I've been thinking about the content of this book for over a decade now, and when I first began putting the ideas to page, it was for my own sake. Once it got rolling though, I really enjoyed the process of making it palatable for others to access.

The second admission is that this book was written for three different reasons. The first two are intertwined, and the third is a bit juvenile. I have been wrestling with my faith, working it out with fear and trembling if you will, for my entire life. So have some other people who are really important to me. We've had our ups and downs, as well as some side to sides, but I have been fortunate because God has placed relational events in my life that have made a huge impact on my faith. What I mean by that is people have been significant forces in the growth, and diminishing of my faith.

That isn't the way it's supposed to be, I know. People are fallible, and will always let you down. The only constant we have is God. I cognitively know this to be true. Unfortunately, I am a fallible human myself, one who has emotions and relies on relationships with others a bit too much sometimes. Anybody with me? Anyways, I wrote this book with those significant people in my life in mind who have had similar experiences. While this project is primarily a glance into my journey, I hope that it will resound with them, both validating their experiences and encouraging them.

That said, a few months ago I had a real crisis of faith. A chapter in my life came to a close, and I was placed in a position where I felt more than a bit helpless, worthless, and lost. I couldn't control the changes in the life of my family (as if I ever really did), and to be perfectly honest, I wasn't sure how we were going to make it. I did what I always do - the "when in danger, when in doubt, run in circles, scream and shout" tango – only to find Jesus' with skin on at every turn.

A family put us up in an extra living space. A friend offered us a job cleaning on the weekends to make a few extra bucks. The Christian School I teach at asked me to come on staff as a campus pastor, with an increase in pay. God met our needs.

While vacuuming floors and cleaning toilets on the weekends, something amazing happened. Keep in mind, I was coming to this new arena after working the week in my role as a teacher and pastor. Both of these hats come with some respect built in. On the other hand, as a toilet man or carpet sucker, I was afforded very little attention by most of the people that met me. If I was noticed, I was generally dismissed with very little courtesy. Oh, how it stung! I think it was most difficult because I have done the same stinking thing! There were exceptions to the rule, of course. I think of them as "the good ones". Folks who would ask how I was doing instead of asking me to come take care of a mess they could have easily cleaned up themselves, and then actively listened to the answer. It really got me thinking about the way I treat everyone in my environment.

I began to share this developing observation with my friend, Peter. He is one of the cooler guys I know, and is constantly challenging me to grow in my relationship with God. He also shared a remarkable insight that God had allowed him to access through experience, and suddenly, as boys often do, we had a competition.

"You outline the idea you have and I'll outline the idea I have and we'll edit each other's work chapter by chapter. You've got two weeks!"

As I write Peter's challenge to me on this digital page, I have yet to see an outline, let alone a chapter of his book. I, on the other hand, could not stand to be last in this friendly, one-sided footrace, and so have completed mine. I know. It's a pretty juvenile reason to write a novelette. I am deeply grateful to Peter, in spite of my immaturity. This has been an important journey for me. I hope it makes others reflect on their attitudes and actions, like it's made me think about my own.

-Jeff

> P.S. Peter, I wonder what my next book will be about? Hmmm…

God cannot be bought.
God will not be boxed in.
God will not be owned by religion.

But God is love,
God is love and
He loves everyone.

White Man
Michael and Lisa Gungor

CHAPTER 1 - BEYOND THE PALE

I was talking with a friend the other day, and he brought up the old colloquialism "beyond the pale". I'd heard the phrase before, generally in reference to those who had done something horrible or who had died, but I had no knowledge of its origin. As he began to share what his research regarding the origin of the phrase had turned up, I was immediately intrigued. Post the conversation, I was spurred on to do a little digital detective work of my own, and what I found was not only immensely interesting, but was also a concrete example of a truth I am coming to understand.
Here's what I found...

The word pale refers to a fence made of sticks that surrounds a dwelling, a group of dwellings, or a larger area of land. Think of Count Dracula, and how he could be taken out via "impaling" with a wooden stake. The word pale is the root from which the term impaling grew.

Now the pale, the fence, was the boundary of safety for the community it surrounded. Those inside were the socially accepted and safe, while those outside were an unknown quantity, considered unsafe until proven otherwise. Further, traveling outside the pale was considered potentially dangerous, as you were moving into an area unknown and uncontrolled by the social norms ascribed to by your group.

Beyond the Pale

Even further, if the community at large decided that you were no longer worthy of being inside the pale, you ran the risk of being ostracized; put outside the pale, away from what was good and safe.

The crux of the phrase is in the idea that going "beyond the pale" is an act of going against social norms, or being labeled "different" by those who are the majority. "Decent" people stay inside the pale. If you're not "decent" then you are an outsider, or run the risk of being forced outside the area of safety and normality.

Let's go back to the original conversation that brought on my dive into aging adage. My friend and I were discussing this phrase in the context of how groups place boundaries around what is acceptable and what isn't, and how people who fall into those two separate categories get relegated to certain circles of influence. As I recall, the idea of condemnation came into the conversation, as it applied to those put outside of the pale. In other words, there are those who, by definition, dwell outside the pale, and there are those who began their life inside the citadel but for one reason or another have been placed outside; the heathen and the condemned, so to speak. Both groups are considered outside social norms, and generally find themselves with diminished influence or privilege. Both, because of nature or choice, find themselves labeled as "other" compared to the majority's "we".

Beyond the Pale

The conversation was a catalyst for me, and was a wonderful, concrete face to a name that has been bouncing around my mind for years. Cogs were whirring, belts were squeaking, and I found a few more puzzle pieces within the dialog that gave me a better overall picture of something I've been trying to focus in on for years. Enter the classic Loony Toons light bulb over my head.

Before I share this little epiphany (ephiphette, perhaps...), I will beg the indulgence of a caveat or two.

1. This is a beginning for me. I have been blinded by being raised as a member of the majority (in many categories) in the United States, and have only begun, over the past decade or two, to have my sight restored.

2. As I have decided to render these ideas to page, I want to make clear that, while I may be somewhat abrupt in my assessment of the function of the Christian "in-group", I am speaking more to myself than to anyone else. If what is here bothers you, then maybe it's not for you...or maybe it is. I found that when these ideas began to worm their way into my understanding, I initially didn't believe them valid, then didn't want them to be valid, then became angry that they were valid.

3. My greatest goal in life is to fulfill the purpose that I was created for. I know that the foundation of this purpose is

relationship, in whatever myriad iterations they may cross my path. I have access to a great relationship model, and hope that some of what I have learned will benefit you with your life purpose fulfillment.

4.   Finally, I could be wrong. Let me rephrase that...I'm sure that some of what I believe right now is skewed. This is a trend I have seen proven over and over again in my life, and though it pains me, it indicates growth. I'm good with growth. Fair warning: The other side of the coin is that I might have some of this right. In either case, I hope this scrap of paper which has blown across your path will give you a moment's pause and cause you to think about the way you view others and why you view them that way.

CHAPTER 2 - THEM AND US

My life has been a blessed one. I was raised in a very stable home, in a small town located in the Northwestern United States. Mom and Dad are wonderful people, my siblings are the best you could ask for, and we were provided a safe and comfortable environment to grow up in. We had the house with white picket fence (actually it was maroon, pressure-treated redwood, but close enough to count). There were moments of slim pickings, but I can never remember going to bed with an empty stomach.

Church played a huge role in my upbringing, as it was the center of our small-town existence. The church family was exactly that, extended family. Crazy deacon uncles who would hold you upside down by an ankle one second and then slip you a quarter in the foyer the next. Aunties with handkerchiefs, shawls, and mints in their purse for keeping little mouths quiet during the service. Older cousins to look up to, and younger ones to put up with. The Senior Pastor was even the quintessential grandfather figure who could do this trick and make his car keys disappear. It was amazing.

Life was good. It was also a bit off.

Can I be blunt? Everyone in my circle of relationships, generally speaking, was just like me. Sure, this was years ago in a very homogenous community, but the unspoken standard

Beyond the Pale

of normality was white, middle or working class, Christian identified, two-parent family, straight, and patriarchal. Not necessarily in that order. The pale was built and manned. Anyone who did not fall into the categories above was "other".

There was "us". There was "them". I find it strange how quickly my young mind accepted the labels and perpetuated the sorting: Those people. The gays. People of color. Catholics. Feminists. Sinners. Them!

I cringe now, just typing this. It reminds me of a visit to my aunt and uncle's home on the east coast. My older cousin had been in a relationship, one which she had hoped would end in a marriage proposal. During our visit the relationship ended, and my cousin was crushed. I was probably eleven or twelve at the time, and had no concept of romantic relationships. Thinking it would be funny, I ran into my cousin's room, where she sat crying, and started chanting "you don't have a boyfriend, you don't have a boyfriend". Nice, eh?! Classy...

I recall, years later and after a difficult relationship dissolution, reflecting on my actions and feeling so ashamed. What had I been thinking?

The fact of the matter is that I was incapable of really understanding the situation and responding in a relevant and appropriate way. I did not have the data needed to do so. The eleven year old boy who made a fool of himself, hurting others in the process, could not understand the depth of his ignorance because he did not have the experience to do so. If I could go back in time to counsel the young me, I would definitely remind him that discretion is the better part of valor. Vigorously, if needed.

When I think of the categorization of those different than me, the neat little pockets I tucked them into during those years, I feel the same shame I did when reflecting on my thoughtless words to my cousin. Turn up the humiliation volume, though. It goes to eleven.

Experience and relationship have broken down many of those misconceptions and presuppositions, and some still come down day by day, but the onion has many layers, my friends. It's hard work to see the flaws in your thinking, and even more difficult to repair them. My ability to build fences is astounding, and as I've begun to recognize the many pales in my life, one which has caused the most pain is in the venue of my relationship with Jesus.

The greatest commandment is to love God with everything you have, and to love your neighbor. I paraphrase here, but I love the way Jesus spoke to the law expert in Dr. Luke's gospel, chapter 10. His not-so-subtle reminder that our question should not be "Who is my neighbor?", but rather, "How can I be a good neighbor?" really strikes me as the answer to one of the biggest barriers we set up as religious people.

Beyond the Pale

Let us review. The story tells us of a man who is robbed, beaten, and left for dead on the side of the road. A spiritual leader and political leader pass him by without helping, but a despised "other" stops to help. Further, this man from "beyond the pale" gives up his transportation, comfort, safety, money, and time to make sure that the victim of the crime is taken care of.

Jesus' final question: "Who is the best neighbor?"

What a question! There is no wiggle room. My four-year-old can answer this one without a moment's pause, or fear that there is a conundrum she may have missed. The question is not one of categories, but one of character.

The problem with my thinking is that I am constantly just like the law expert who asked Jesus the question. Instead of trying to find ways to be a good neighbor to everyone, I'm searching for a "decent" neighbor to be good to. Beyond that, I'm trying to construct a neighborhood in which everyone's house looks exactly the same as my own.

Jesus sets that mentality on its ear! It's like calling a building a church. Quit looking for good neighbors and be one! Quit "going to church" and be a productive part of the body!

Did the Samaritan ask about the wounded man's religious affiliation or sexual preference? Was his marital status an issue in providing him with the help he needed to survive? Or flip it around - did the Samaritan's status as a divorcee exclude him from being able to serve? Did his dependence on federal aid disqualify his actions as neighborly? Did his ethnicity or faith in any way detract from his ability to be used by God?

I wonder if the distinction that we construct between "saved" and "unsaved" holds the same meaning for the Creator of us all? We generally make it a club thing: you're either in or out. As a dad of young children, I think about how I view my little ones. I pray they will grow up to have a relationship with me, but if they choose not to, does that exclude them from my love? Will they no longer be my daughters?

Not a chance. I remember those tear-blurred newborn fingers and toes I counted so carefully. The tiny nurse who tried to take my daughter away to clean her got an earful and a companion for the entirety of the bath. Their first steps, first words, laughs, tears...I know those little ones and there is nothing I wouldn't do for them. A younger me would have said it in a heartbeat. An older, more experienced me now knows it to be true. I would die for those girls.

How much more does God know the most strange of my neighbors? How much more does he love them. For the sake of the "worst" of us, he chose to die one of the more excruciating and demeaning deaths imaginable. He didn't just say it. He didn't just know it. He did it. Yes, even for a white, middle class guy like me.

Psalm 139 really does a great job of putting my thinking in the right path. Here's what I do: I read the passage as though it is being said about someone who is drastically different than I am. It's wonderful to know that the Creator of the universe knows me so intimately, but it is a good reminder that He also knows those who I have a hard time connecting to just as completely. There is no difference, in Jesus' eyes, between them and me.

The Pale: Us and Them
The Truth: We construct the walls between those who are different than we are, while Jesus breaks them down.

CHAPTER 3 - JUXTAPOSED JESUS

The memory of falling asleep at my grandparent's home in Coquille, Oregon is such a pleasant and comforting recollection. Whether on the living room floor or couch, the sound of the grandfather clock and the smell of dish soap, cookies, and sawdust were the perfect anesthetic for a crazy little boy. There was a sculpture on the wall of that room that depicted Jesus praying in the garden of Gethsemane, which now hangs in my living room. When Grandma and Grandpa "passed their final exams", one of the things that got moved down the family chain to me was this tableau in three dimensions. It is noteworthy to me for a couple of reasons.

First, I recall studying the rendering as a child and noting that the artist used a black-hued medium to construct the piece. I'm sure the reason was because the depiction represents Jesus praying at night, but even as a child I understood that Jesus' ethnicity was not the same as my own and that he probably didn't have the same skin tone or facial features that I did. I remember carefully running my hands along his face and hands and wondering if this might have been the real color of his skin.

While most of the facial features of the Jesus in the work are Eurocentric in nature, one feature is not. Whether the sculpture meant to or not, the nose of the figure is much wider than those in most iconography that I had seen around me. The nose lends to the difference in such a manner that the young me found it a place to begin to question the skinny, white, long-haired icons constantly seen around me. Beyond that, it ushered in a beginning of the belief that difference does not mean danger, but instead could mean salvation.

Jumping to the present, I was reading an article produced by the magazine *Popular Mechanics* in which a forensic anthropologist constructed a bust of what an average man from Jesus' geographic locale and time might have looked like. Looking at a photo of the construction, I was shocked to see similarities to the sculpture now hanging in my living room, and even more to the mental picture I had constructed so many years before. Even so, it battled with the multilayered images of that Eurocentric Jesus so prevalent in Western religious iconography.

As I've reflected over the years, this internal struggle of the juxtaposed Jesus pushed my thinking even further. If we, as a family of believers in the deity of Jesus, can't graphically represent Him in an accurate manner, what else do we believe about Him that is fallacy? If we find it most comfortable to change a simple thing like a picture in a way that better matches what we seen inside our pale, what else are we misrepresenting? God is in the details, so in what details have we omitted a true picture of Him?

Juxtaposed Jesus

I've heard it proposed in many a church service over my years of attendance, but there is a question that bears repeating. "What would you do if Jesus walked through the doors of the place where you gather to worship?" Or, even better, "What would you do if a Middle Eastern Jesus knocked at your door?" What would be your initial impulse?

My heart hurts when I think of what mine would be. In this post 9/11 era of our world, my first impulse would be fear. Not because I think that every person of Middle-Eastern decent is a terrorist, but rather because I wouldn't recognize the person at the door. I do not have a label for them inside the pale I've constructed in my thinking about them. While I have a relationship with people of differing cultures and backgrounds, my unease when encountering an unknown member of this ethnicity blatantly shows a pale that I need some work deconstructing. It also shows that I need to further my relationship with my creator.

But how would Jesus react to my church family? How would he feel if he were to encounter me? My initial response is a reversal of the famous movie *Guess Who's Coming to Dinner*, with Jesus sitting down at my dining room table and finding the company and conversation lacking. Who am I, an unrefined Gentile, trying to show the Master of the universe even a modicum of the hospitality He deserves. My best just doesn't cut it.

Beyond that, his instruction states that the way I treat those who are "other" parallels the way I treat him. There is no separation. The off color joke, the exclusion because of my discomfort, the white lie to negate obligation- they're all done to someone who recognizes what they are and the selfish motives behind them. Ouch!

Are you ready for "Ouch, Part 2"?

If there is any being in the history of eternity that has a right to treat another as less than, or other, it is Yahweh in regards to us. His perfection is unique. Our imperfection is universal. Our sin put us beyond the pale, while His inability to sin makes him the only refuge we have. How do you spell "dichotomy"?

Fortunately, the Bible is very clear on how Jesus reacts to our company, whether it is viewed as individual or as a group. I don't need to relegate my negative perspectives on how westernized religion has gone away from the spirit of the law, or how my shortcomings are a glaring, red letter A on my shirtfront to His perspective. If I seek His kingdom first and try to do the right thing according to his example, I'm good! In seeking His kingdom, and being righteous, the question then becomes how to do so in relationship to others.

Who do I associate with? Who will I not associate with, and why? Where does the rubber meet the road practically, or what am I doing to better know the Jesus I see every day?

Juxtaposed Jesus

The Pale: "Other" equals danger.
The Truth: "Other" equals Jesus.

Beyond the Pale

CHAPTER 4 - BATTLING BIAS

Okay. So let's just jump into it. I know the place where I intend to go with the next few lines is one where many readers will vehemently disagree. Less than ten years ago, I would have been a dissenter as well. I was a dissenter, in fact.

Here's the scoop. I returned to college after a brief ten year break as a missionary and children's minister to complete my BA. One of the entry level classes at the state run school I attended was meant to introduce the learner to the paradigm of oppression. It was a required class, and my initial thoughts were that it sounded interesting. That changed quickly.

I knew there was going to be a variety of struggles upon the completion of the first night of class. There were some glaring discrepancies between me, the newly instated college student, and the rest of the class. I was the only white male in the class, and only one of five or six European-Americans total. There were only four men in the class. I was the oldest person in attendance, including the professor who was a middle-twenties, crew cut and outspoken lesbian. The alarm klaxons were sounding: Other! Other! Other!

One of the first readings assigned was a paper written by Peggy McIntosh entitled "White Privilege: Unpacking the Invisible Knapsack". Oh, how it rankled me. The big idea in the piece that just got my goat was the idea that I, a God fearing, loving, minister of the gospel could possibly be

Beyond the Pale

oppressing others without even knowing that I was. Further, the author posited that this oppression actually acted as a springboard for my privilege. By wanting to help "better" those who are "other" than me, I was actually only helping myself because as they rise in privilege, my springboard rises accordingly.

The definition of what makes one "better" was also called into question. As a member of the majority, bettering one who was other equated to making them more like the majority. More like me. It was suggested that I was trying to save the "savages" by helping them change their ways, replacing them with decency, and allowing them inside the fence.

I argued. I got angry. I fought the very thought that any of this could be remotely true. Let me share with you the mantra my professor and most of my peers plied me with throughout the journey of the class.

"Of course you don't believe in it. You can't see it like we can. It's nearly invisible to those who have it. It's invisible privilege."

And, as I really began to critically reflect on the things I take for granted as a white, middle class, male, I found validity in the assertions. Bandages that are "flesh" color match my skin tone. I have never had to wonder if the reason I didn't get a job was because of the interviewer's disdain of my sex, ethnicity, or sexual preference. I can hold any political view I want without being considered a cultural outsider. I can use brash language, wear ratty clothing, and not respond to correspondence without it being attributed to bad morals, poverty, or illiteracy.

My blinders were coming off, but I still had a fence post or two up my sleeve.

My next argument was more of a lateral movement than acquiescence. Sure, maybe I had an advantage because I was part of the majority, but it wasn't my fault. Wasn't there reverse oppression as well? I had heard often in my circle of relationships about people who had been treated poorly because they were white. What about that?

My professor, who is still a friend, put it to me in a way that stripped the remnants of my pale and left me open to really see the truth of what it was to look from the outside in. Oppression can only be levered by those with the power to wield it. Logic took it from there.

How do I become a person who does not, consciously or unconsciously, rely on my majority privilege to better my life through the lessening of others? Jesus' response is my favorite. Want to be the greatest in my kingdom? Become the servant of everyone you meet. Don't try to make them be like you...you act like me and lay down your life for them.

What if they are an overbearing atheist?

Love them with a servant's heart.

What if they are a confirmed pagan who will never change?

Beyond the Pale

Love them with a servant's heart.

What if they lessen who I am within my circle of relationships through our acquaintance or through their actions?

Yup, you got it. Love them with a servant's heart.

You see, the big lesson for me in all of this is that there is no normal. Normal is a generality constructed to convey privilege to some and retract it from others. It is a pale, or series of pales, that allow only those with power to maintain their power at the expense of the rest.

Why am I sermonizing about social dynamics? Perhaps you are not part of the majority, speaking in terms of ethnicity, gender, etc. I am taking one thing for granted, and for those who do not fall into this category, I apologize for my assumption. Here it is. If you identify as a Christian, you are a member of the "spiritual" majority here in the US. Varying studies place Christians, in their myriad shapes, sizes, and brands at around 75% of the population. That's three out of four people, people!

Armed with that knowledge, do you think that there might be a little unseen privilege in the pack on your back? Perhaps this question is a bit premature, as you are still struggling with the idea that invisible privilege is a reality at all. I'm going to push on through anyway.

How do you think of those who are not Christian? Are you the angry brother or overjoyed father when viewing the prodigal? When a group complains about a Christian holiday celebration or a religious symbol in a public place, where does your mind go? Are you immediately overwhelmed with the need to love them with a servant's heart, or do you reach for a post-hole digger?

We all have bias for or against someone, no matter how you identify yourself. Bias is just an unfair preference or dislike of something, or in this case, someone. Bias against things we have little knowledge of is just a natural offshoot of ignorance. Hold on, hold on...I'm not insulting anyone's mama here. I'm just saying that without taking the time to get to know someone who is different from you, and your perception of normal, you're going to make assumptions that aren't necessarily true. The greater the divide, the greater the schism between truth and presupposition. The greater the bias.

Am I promoting a "don't knock it 'till you've tried it" mentality here? Not at all. There are some clear guidelines in God's Word as to what is good and what is not. On the other hand, there are also a lot of things, and even more so people, that we take as read when we have very little data to support our assumptions.

Want to get rid of some of the bias in your life? Go build a relationship with someone who is from outside your pale. It won't, generally, kill you. In fact, it might, actually, start to heal you.

Beyond the Pale

The Pale: I have no bias.
The Truth: Everybody does.

CHAPTER 5 - TOLERANCE

Have you read the chapter title? Just so you know, I'll try not to rant. Maybe I'll succeed. A little.

Tolerance is defined as the ability or willingness to tolerate something, in particular the existence of behaviors or opinions that one does not necessarily agree with. I tolerate spinach. That is, as long as it doesn't try to marry my daughter. Once that happens, all bets are off. The connotation behind the word is reminiscent of a particularly unstable, snow covered mountain side. Beautiful on the surface, but one wrong move and all those flakes will rain down destruction on anything in their path.

I wrote a poem when I was a teen, and entitled it "Christian Pride". The deep-as-a-puddle premise was that Christians were like lions, looking to pick off the weak or ill in their own ranks. Oddly enough I wrote the poem after a few well-meaning souls in our church family decided to take me aside for an edification conference regarding how Christians should dress. My acid washed, holey-kneed jeans and matching jacket were a bit to risqué for the small town Pentecostal crowd, evidentially. The paradox of the situation was that I really loved and respected the opinions of the lecturers, while at the same time I hated the fact that they couldn't get past my exterior to see who I was becoming. My style did not change. They tolerated me, or I, at least, felt that way. I began to ride the fence.

Please don't misunderstand. I would have probably ridden the fence whether they had accepted me or rejected me. I am a natural born skeptic, in spite of the faith-filled family I am surrounded by. Would the fence ride have been a shorter one had those church family members chosen to pick their battles a little more carefully? I'm guessing yes.

We are all looking for acceptance. I am no different than every other human being who has ever walked the earth in this respect. One of the great questions of life is that which surrounds the need to be a good person. In one form or another we all need the pat on the shoulder or the 'atta boy letting us know we are part of something and needed.

We also need to know that the life we are living is one that matters. I want to know that my thoughts are important, my dreams and wishes have significance, my rights are considered, and that my beliefs have value. When I feel validated, whatever the reason, I am empowered to validate. I don't want a band of "yes men" following me around, but I do want to know that someone is willing to listen and consider.

On the other hand I, for one, am not looking to be tolerated. Yet I find myself treating others that way. The most difficult interactions for me are usually the ones that occur with church family members, those who are most familiar to

Tolerance

me. Again, life imitating cliché: Familiarity breeding contempt. Allow me to give you a few fer instances...

There are those who consistently have trials or tribulations of varying sorts and when asked how they are doing will relay, in detail, exactly how difficult life is. So I tolerate them. And avoid them when at all possible.

Then there are those folks who have to put their nose into every little discussion that occurs. They are the referees who want to make sure that all sides have their opinions heard and that everyone gets a fair shake. As if meetings aren't long enough as it is...

What about the ones that bounce from church to church, looking for the right fit, but never quite finding it? Here one week, gone the next. I tolerate them.

How about those people who always are quick to point out the flaws in the church, or in me for that matter? I know that we're not perfect, but God don't make no junk, right!? I got rid of the acid washed jeans years ago! Barely tolerable.

And then there are the ones who never get involved in anything. They warm a pew on Sunday, but will barely respond when you talk to them, and won't sign up to serve in any ministry. I'm never quite sure if they are shy, disinterested, or condescending.

Finally, there are those "fixers" who always have some sort of charity case they are trying to help. I mean, I know that Jesus was always looking to meet the needs of those around him, but shouldn't they pace themselves? We've only got so much coming in through the offerings and tithes. It's a church, not a savings and loan.

Just so we're clear, this is a bit tongue-in-cheek. Only a bit though. Often, I find myself rolling and eye or giving my wife "the look" when I show my great character by tolerating those who fall into the categories above. The thing is, tolerance is nowhere near the model Jesus provided us. I may think I'm doing folks a favor by putting up with their shortcomings, when in fact, Jesus is lovingly walking through the crowd saying,

Blessed are the poor in spirit,
    For theirs is the kingdom of heaven.
Blessed are those who mourn,
    For they shall be comforted.
Blessed are the meek,
    For they shall inherit the earth.
Blessed are those who hunger and thirst for righteousness,
    For they shall be filled.
Blessed are the merciful,
    For they shall obtain mercy.
Blessed are the pure in heart,
    For they shall see God.
Blessed are the peacemakers,
    For they shall be called sons of God.

Tolerance

Blessed are those who are persecuted for righteousness' sake,
   For theirs is the kingdom of heaven.
Blessed are you when they revile and persecute you, and say all kinds of evil against you falsely for My sake. Rejoice and be exceedingly glad, for great is your reward in heaven, for so they persecuted the prophets who were before you.

I call them a whiner, Jesus offers comfort.
I call them wishy-washy, Jesus offers fulfillment.
I call them slackers, Jesus offers them the earth.
I call them busy bodies, Jesus call them His kids.

    In spite of my finger pointing at those who put me in the "tolerate seat" as a young Christian, I find myself playing the Pharisee. I'm the guy who was forgiven an insurmountable debt, but in the next instant smacks another for not paying back chump change. Jesus proclaims a blessing over those who are "other", whether inside or outside my circle of relationships. He doesn't *tolerate* the flawed, he **accepts** them. He doesn't put up with their idiosyncrasies, He loves in spite of them. Jesus dug my acid washed jeans!
    A few years back there was a t-shirt making the rounds which stated "Love Sees No Color". I really liked the sentiment and the idea behind it, but now that I've had a while to ruminate on it, I don't think that it was quite right.

Beyond the Pale

I think that love sees every color. There isn't color that love doesn't revel in. Across the spectrum of every possible difference humanity has, love sees it all. Love dances with the vividly joyous and cradles the blandly bereft. From the lowest to highest caste, the most unrepentant sinner to saint, the brilliant to broken, love sees it all.

From my greatest achievement to my most hidden handicap, love sees.

And guess what? Love accepts.

The Pale: I tolerate difference.
The Truth: Jesus accepts me.

CHAPTER 6 - ORGANISM VS. ORGANIZATION

While spending time with some friends at a birthday celebration, I was party to a very unique occurrence (no pun intended...sorry). As the member of our group whose birthday we were celebrating sat at the head of the table, we began to share what it was about him that we found unique and outstanding. Person by person told of the impact that the birthday boy had on their lives, sterling character traits he embodied, and relationship anecdotes that were meaningful and important.

I was fortunate enough to be early in the rotation and was transfixed by the sharing that followed. In the span of a little more than an hour, eight of us shared corroborative testimony of the life of a man who had changed us for the better. His willingness to serve each of those sharing had given them a feeling of value and belonging that transcended their dysfunction. His interest in each witness was evidenced through the actions and words he had accumulatively put into each life represented around the circle. Though some shared for a longer time than others, and some were more verbose than others, the theme that emerged was underpinned clearly with the fact that what was said was merely the tip of an iceberg.

Beyond the Pale

The event started my wheels turning. As I sat there listening to the words of those around me, I wondered how similar this gathering was to one of the many that happened thousands of years ago, on another continent. An overlay blanketed the group in my mind, and I started reconciling members of my group with members of another well-known group. I, of course, was "The Doubter". Rocky was right up close, next to "the teacher", and John was on his left. The other "Son of Thunder" sat next to me, as did the doctor. Both Mary and Martha were in attendance. The resolution wasn't perfect, but it fit.

And here's the clincher...this group gathered was ministry staff for the church I am a part of. And it was our weekly staff meeting. Further, the man whose birthday we were celebrating was our lead pastor. Let me be clear - it wasn't a disingenuous outpouring of platitudes, nor was it a rote recitation of expected pleasantries that accompanied a specific event. Somehow, that instant in time captured a truth about the character of the man celebrated, while additionally echoing a much larger truth about the paradoxical power of purposefully tearing down walls that separate "us" from "them".

That larger truth seems to stem from the idea that humanity, while arguably organized, is not an organization. I know I'm speaking semantically here, but roll with me for a moment. Humanity does not equal organization. Rather, humanity better equates to an organism. The analogy that Jesus uses is that of a body. I like that one.

My wife recently had a problem with her debit card. I was sitting on the couch, watching a movie, when my phone had a message pop up on it. The message informed me that my wife had just purchased a $500 stereo system from an online vender, and the money had been taken from our account. My wife was asleep in bed, so I was fairly sure that the message was wrong about her purchase. I quickly jumped on the computer, checked our account, and low and behold, it was $500 smaller than my records showed!

Let me kill the suspense here and just state that my wife had not been online shopping in her sleep, although that would have made an excellent story as well. Somehow, her identity had been stolen, and a fraudulent purchase had been made using her card. I went into damage control mode, beginning with a call to our bank.

They politely gave me the brush-off! I'm not joking here. The irritatingly pleasant woman, who I was tolerant of, nicely told me that there was nothing she could do for me until the purchase was finalized through the bank. I asked if that meant that I still had access to the "pending", but missing $500. The answer was a negative.

I went proactive. The name of the online vender was listed, so I gave them a call. They were awesome! The order hadn't shipped, so they were able to cancel it and process a refund. The spectacular gentleman representing them apologized for not being able to immediately refund my missing, pending money, as the process would have to go through...my bank.

I called my bank back, thinking they would be grateful for my effort, doing their job, but was surprised to find that the soonest they would be able to adjust my account would be 3-5 working days. Three working days later, my pending funds were absent, as were they after five working days. My calls to the bank were numerous. Their pleasant deflections were equivalent. It took thirteen days for them to replace my not-quite-stolen money!

This story has a topper, as well. A day after my funds were returned, the credit from the online company was somehow processed into my account. I was suddenly $500 wealthier than I should have been. In spite of my perceived mistreatment, I called the bank to let them know about the accounting error. I was tempted to empty the account so that I could let them know I would be able to return their funds in three to five working days, but opted not to.
The topper? Here it is:
The excess money was processed out of my account within minutes, even before the end of the phone conversation.
Ah, the intimacy of organization!

Seriously, though, I think that the dichotomous examples of my banking experience and the church ministry staff interaction do a great job of representing the difference between organism and organization.

Organization seeks to forward an overarching agenda, focusing on the benefit that its components can bring to the structure, and ridding itself of those who do not. Organism has an overarching agenda of caring and nurturing its members, sending sustenance and protection to where it is needed most, while not endangering the whole. In other words, a crippled or malfunctioning part of an organization is generally done away with. A sick or injured part of the body is babied and cared for until it is better, or until it gets the attention needed by a doctor.

Organization sees its environment as a place for expansion and growth, competing to survive above others who may be trying to corner the same market. Organism lives cooperatively within its environment, understanding that reciprocity and temperance is the secret to long-term success.

Organization's highest goal is growth of assets. Organism's highest goal is health and safety of offspring.

I was chatting with my brother about this comparison the other night, and he made a great point. His take on the whole organism vs. organization was one tangent I hadn't even contemplated, in regards to the efficiency and complexity of each. An organization can only be as complex and efficient as its organizers, while an organism, at least with our current knowledge, seems to become more and more complex and self-correcting the more closely you scrutinize it. He is the vine, we are the branches. He is the head, we are the body. There is a signature of the Divine in organism that can only be shoddily copied by organization.

If we are a part of that Christ-minded organism, shouldn't our actions reflect his direction, his emphasis? I want to be part of the living, breathing, interdependent whole that functions to care for its members, to live in harmony with my neighbors, and care for its young and weak.

The Pale: We belong to the group.
The Truth: We belong to Him.

CHAPTER 7 - REBEL IN SANDALS

The fear of being placed beyond the pale is one the greatest motivators with reference to the individual's drive to assimilate. We all want to be decent, right?! We all want to be accepted. The problem is that the rules that dictate who is accepted inside the fence are not always righteous.

So we do wrong in the name of decency. Sorry, let me not share this responsibility by using the royal "we". When my goal is acceptance of those within the pale, I often do wrong in the name of decency. But it isn't always a Patrick McGoohan, *The Village*, sort of thing. If only it was! This trek, for me, is much more of a parallel, Bunyanesque, By-Path meadow. It's a fine differentiation, but the matter of a fraction of degree is enough to change our envisioned destination. I'm not trying to do the wrong thing. I'm just not doing the right thing.

It's ironic. I am so quick to see the villainy of the Pharisee that I need a seat belt and a roll bar - The belt for the speed and the bar for the impending crash. The caricature I see here is one directly out of a beautiful visual Jesus used while teaching a large group of people. Before I share the story, let me point out that some of the people in the crowd were very versed in the law of the scripture, academics of local note probably. Skeptics. Smart 'uns.

Beyond the Pale

Matthew chapter seven presents a Jesus I love in one breath, and fear in the next. Here we see the presentation of ultimate acceptance and steel-cored rebellion. The Message presents one of my favorite renditions of the moment. It says, [1-5] "Don't pick on people, jump on their failures, criticize their faults— unless, of course, you want the same treatment. That critical spirit has a way of boomeranging. It's easy to see a smudge on your neighbor's face and be oblivious to the ugly sneer on your own. Do you have the nerve to say, 'Let me wash your face for you,' when your own face is distorted by contempt? It's this whole traveling road-show mentality all over again, playing a holier-than-thou part instead of just living your part. Wipe that ugly sneer off your own face, and you might be fit to offer a washcloth to your neighbor."

The dramatic music swells. A deep and gravelly voiceover cuts in. You can visualize your own video clips as we go. Just know that I'm too often the star of this feature.

"In a world where men with logs sticking out of their eyes try to instruct their neighbor on how to remove the dust from his own..."

Okay, so I'm being a bit silly. I tend to do that when dancing around a lesson that is hard to palette. It's the whole "spoon full of sugar making the medicine go down" strategy.

So Jesus, speaking to the group, lovingly points out that often we are quick to see the trivial error of other's ways while completely ignoring the crippling ones in our own. Self-perseverance through transference: He did it first, or she did it worse.

I'm sure that those listening to this message reacted to it in a variety of ways. Think about it - the crowd at the teaching was a made up of transients who had no problem picking up stakes and following the crowd, families who were treating this like an outing, addicted and abandoned folks who were in need of healing, haughty scholars who were there to look down their nose at and challenge this upstart...a gradient of humanity assembled in a single venue. All of them had a similar problem.

Jesus hits on a universal in that moment. He tells them that their focus should not be on the differences between themselves and those they consider "other", but rather on the difference between the person they could be, one that is in harmony with their Creator, and the person that they actually are. He says to this crowd, He says to you and me, "Hey, log-eye! You're all in the same boat, here. I am the only safe place, yet you compare yourself to others and build these fences separating yourself from each other and, ultimately, from me!" You'd think that when Jesus points out the beam that is blinding us, we'd pull it out and burn it rather than using it to build a larger barrier.

Beyond the Pale

How does this look, practically speaking? Let me tell you...

A good friend of mine, Yvonne, recently had an experience that nails the spirit of this lesson on the head, in my estimation. In her neighborhood, as in many neighborhoods, there is certain resident. You know the one I'm talking about, right!? People coming in and out at all hours. Police showing up on a consistent basis. Loud parties and even louder fights. Yup...that neighbor.

All the normal, good neighbors tsk-tsk and talk about how it's too bad that there has to be that element in their generally safe environment. Stories are shared about the different escapades this resident has been involved with. Though living next door, this neighbor is definitely "beyond the pale".

Yvonne was a bit surprised one day when she felt led by God to talk to the neighbor. I love the way she described her initial response. "You've got to be kidding, God! There is no way I'm going there. It might not be safe. What will the neighbors think if they see me talking to her? I don't know her. What if she flips out on me?"

Strangely, all her excuses didn't change the gentle pressure she felt to talk to the neighbor. Again, I loved her description of how she tried to deflect the request. "Okay, God, the next time I see her, I'll talk to her." Yvonne knew that it had been months, if not years since she'd seen the neighbor. She could appease Dad, while keeping the odds in her favor.

Guess what happened the next day? Uh-huh. My friend is driving home and who should she see standing on the side of the road? The neighbor. At this point, Yvonne told me that she knew if she didn't stop and talk with the girl, she would be directly disobeying her Heavenly Father. Not something she takes lightly. So she pulls over to the side of the road, jumps out of the car, and walks up to her neighbor.

None of her fears about interacting with the neighbor came to fruition. In fact, the opposite happened. Yvonne kindly told the girl that, even though she had no idea about where her faith life might be, she needed to tell her that Jesus loved her. Wherever she was at, good or bad, Jesus accepted her and thought of her as his kid.

The girl broke down and began to cry.

Her life was a wreck. There were relationship problems, self-esteem issues, and all sorts of brokenness. Two weeks before, she had miscarried. Two nights before, a couple of women had forced their way into her home and beaten her up in front of her young child. She was sad, hurt, and feeling helpless. She told Yvonne that people had talked to her about God before, but she had never believed He loved her until she heard it from Yvonne.

Beyond the Pale

    Wait. Did you get that? I repeat, people had talked to her about God before but she hadn't believed in the truth of their words until she heard it from Yvonne. Wow.

    Well, it gets better. As the conversation continued, the girl began to share that there actually was one other person who had shared God's love with her that she had believed was sincere. There was this little old man who she would see consistently at a local store and who was always telling her how much Jesus loved her. She told Yvonne that he even gave her a bible once, and that she looked forward to seeing him because of the way she felt after talking to him. She felt like she was important, that what she was going through was cared about, and that what she thought mattered. The girl said it was strange because it had been an unusually long time since she'd seen the gentleman, and she wondered where he was.

    As the girl described the tall, bushy-browed man to my friend, and as Yvonne shared the story with me, our eyes began to fill up with tears. I'm tearing up as I write this now. Yvonne knew who the man was. He was one of the pillars of the church we attend. I do not mean this in a trite or cliché way. This man was solid, generous, and genuine in every way. His faith in God was not pushy, but was evident in the way he interacted with everyone around him. He was roughhewn, but if there was a need he could serve, he did. He walked the walk, and it spoke volumes.

Rebel in Sandals

He has also gone to be with his Heavenly Father. Around the time that this man got to go home, Yvonne began to feel the push to talk to her neighbor, ignorant of the connection. She shared the fact of his death with the girl, who reacted in an interesting way. Her response, while disappointed that that she didn't get to say goodbye, was not one of sorrow. Instead, she was insistent that this man knew that she needed to hear about God's love, and had asked God to send Yvonne to her.

Again, did you get that!? Yvonne's willingness to be obedient, in spite of the trek into unknown terrain allowed her to be used by God.

While the girl's theology may be a bit muddled, the outcome is not. Yvonne chose to step outside a pale in her life, following in the rock-n-roll sandal prints of Jesus. She wasn't the first to follow the path, but instead got to take over where a "pale-ignoring" Christ follower had finished his hike. And, in her own words, the dividends of loving with a servant's heart were overwhelming. In spite of her "bratty" attitude (Yvonne's words again, not mine) her loving heavenly father blessed her socks off while allowing her to be His hand outstretched to someone in need. She got to know her maker that much better, and the blessing received was exponentially greater than the effort expended.

The Pale : At least I'm not as bad as them...
The Truth: Log-eye, you need a doctor.

Beyond the Pale

CHAPTER 8 - BABY JESUSES

When I was a kid, and King Jimmy was the only "real" translation of the bible, there was a certain passage that initially threw me for a loop. My 1980's slang just didn't mesh with the 1600's English. The whole "suffer the little children" thing...what was with that? Totally not cool, dude!

My dad was quick to explain that the term *suffer*, in this case, had nothing to do with pain or sadness, but rather with the act of permission. Now that I'm older, and modern translations make the passage more accessible for kids of all ages, I still have the good ol' KJV in my long-term storage. It's really the second half of the verse that applies to my strand of thinking here, though.

"Forbid them not, for such is the kingdom of heaven."

Does that mean that Jesus' Kingdom, God's Kingdom, is like one made up of the same rules and regulations that govern a group of children? Could that be the case? Might the social dynamics of children be a valid representation of the way that we are supposed to interact with others (and those who are "other")?

I say yes. My experience of growing up in a diversity-challenged environment led, at least in part, to some erroneous presuppositions. Not initially, though. It took time without the benefit of diverse, realia-based relationship learning before it became easy to incorrectly quantify and qualify people who were different than those who were within my pale. I regarded them as "less than" because there was not a concrete representation to defend against the construction, and I did so in ways that I would never have considered doing to those who were present and accessible.

Skip 30 years forward in time. My three progeny have been raised in a very diverse environment, specifically on a college campus in California. Their experience growing up is quite different than mine in a lot of ways, to say the least. Our family has been exposed to such a beautiful variety of humanity over the past ten years, and my little ones have learned to interact with others in those varied conditions.

One of the things that I most admire in my daughters is their relationship building skills. They've learned the majority of these from their mama, who is not just my best friend, but an incredibly friendly lady. They have such a diverse group of friends, ranging in age, gender, ethnicity, socio-economic status, religious affiliation, etc. They recognize difference in their circle of relationships, but they accept those differences as strengths and pathways, not strangeness and road blocks.

And my girls love Jesus. They accept "other" so much more naturally than I will ever be able to, and I see more of Jesus in them because of it. Now, why is that? What is the piece that has allowed them to access so easily the relational sightedness and comfort that I must work so hard to grasp? My only response is that it must be a learned behavior.

My wife was raised in a military family that moved very often, causing her and her sisters to either learn to make friends quickly, or not at all. They chose quick. When her family finally settled, it was in a town that had a very diverse population, one where my wife was able to build relationships with all kinds of folks. In fact, there was not a large enough representation of European-American students in one of the local schools, so my wife was bussed in, with a few other white kids, during her eighth grade year. While there were some challenges for her, the benefits greatly outweighed any detriments. She brought a unique amalgamation of these two experiences to our marriage and child rearing table, and I have benefitted from it so much. Needless to say, so have my girls.

I want to be clear on this. I believe that original sin pushes all of us into the reality of separateness from God and, by proxy, divides us from true relationship with anyone. Not one of us is inherently good. Our nature, at its core, is a self-seeking one. In order to be in a truly beneficial relationship with another, we must first be firmly rooted in relationship with our heavenly father, as that is the only means by which to obtain the power to truly be self-sacrificing.

Back to the question of my daughters' ease of relationship with those different than them, I think that, while their nature

Beyond the Pale

at base is a self-centered one, through the nurturing of Jesus they are able to accept and love. Sure, one of the big "Jesus with skin on" examples they have is my wife, and I'd like to think that I've played a part as well, but the truth of the matter is that the Love they have (note the capitol "L") is a direct product of the power they tap into.

They are a window for me through which I can view my Creator. They are little Jesuses to me. When He told his disciples that kids are a model of his kingdom, I think that one of the things Jesus was referring to was their lack of bias and skewed evaluation of difference. Their willingness to accept and love is boundless, bravely and whole-heartedly proffered. Little ones are not easily offended, and forgive between heartbeats. They search for bridges of similarity rather than building fences of dispute. They laugh together, then fight, forgive, and frolic again within the stretch of an afternoon. Just like the kingdom that Jesus offers each of us.

I want that! I'm determined to get that! When my nature cries "different" I want it put in the ground and have the Christ who now lives in me emerge, hand outstretched. I want to begin relationships with others openheartedly, with a patented "Wanna' play?" and no other agenda or preconception. I want the differences of others to be something I rely on for better understanding of my Dad, not something to further cage me into the cycle of narcissism.

Baby Jesuses

Again, I have a model to follow. Actually, I have more than one, in this instance. One walked this earth two millennium ago. Three are walking it next to me daily. Who would have thought that such little feet would wear such large shoes? I struggle to fill them, but it's a good fight.

The Pale: No one can change human nature.
The Truth: Jesus can change anything.

Beyond the Pale

CHAPTER 9 - R.E.S.P.E.C.T.

In searching for ways to best live out a pale diminishing life, I am so glad to have come across 1 Peter 2:17. As my grandpa would have lovingly said, it's one of those "keep it simple" passages that was written for a thick-headed, motor-mouth like me. Here it is:

"Honor everyone."

There is more to it than that, of course. The scripture tells us to love our fellow Christians, fear God, and honor our rulers. The first one though, honoring everyone, is so well suited for my concrete mind, I'm pretty sure that it was written for me. It's first on the list. Honor everyone. Let's break it down...

"Honor", the verb, means "to regard with great respect". Great. Okay, so "respect", the verb, means to have due regard for the feelings, rights, wishes, or traditions of another. "Due regard" meaning "timely thought". Finally, we have "everyone", which is the noun meaning "every person". Every person.

Scripture is telling us to take time to think about the feelings, rights, wishes, or traditions of every person. Honor everyone.

Beyond the Pale

I feel Otis and hear Aretha, brothers and sisters.

The passage isn't saying we have to agree with everyone. It's also not saying that we have to have intricate knowledge of every people group in the world. It is saying we need to be focused on honoring those in our circle of relationships whether they are inside our pale or not, and on following the Golden Rule, treating everyone the way we would want to be treated. Too simple? Maybe in concept. Practice is a whole other ball of wax...

One of my original forays into becoming "de-picketed" came in the form of joining YWAM for a trip to Fiji at the age of 19. What a trip! Before we left, we were warned by our leaders to be very careful with our words while staying with the locals during the trip. We were instructed not to directly compliment articles of clothing, items in homes, jewelry, etc. The reason we were cautioned to guard our tongues was because, in the culture, a compliment was treated like a request, and requests were paramount when showing hospitality. In other words, if you complimented an item, people felt obligated to give it to you.

This assertion was almost immediately put to the test. One member of the group unthinkingly commented on how cool one of the Fijian's knit beanies was. Without pause, the man removed it and gave it to the commenter, thanking him for the compliment. Fortunately, my mission teammate had the presence of mind not to refuse the gift, as it would have been considered an insult. We learned later that the man who had given the hat had received it as part of his recently deceased brother's possessions. My mission teammate was mortified. His idle words had forced a host to give up a sentimentally priceless article. His ignorance created offense, and pain.

If I am to honor everyone, which seems a VERY DIFFICULT challenge, then I have to have at least some knowledge of everyone within my geographic locale. I have to know their rights, feelings, traditions, and wishes so that I show them due regard. I love the fact that this simple dictate, honor everyone, implies that the focus of this honor must be known. To give everyone the honor due, you have to know about them. You can only generally "honor everyone" without some sort of relationship.

Let me clarify this with another story. I am, at heart, a practical being who needs to understand the function as well as process. For my entire life I was raised in an environment that taught me "Jesus died for the world". That is how I viewed it. We were all in the same boat, up the same creek, and we all were missing the paddle. Without a savior, we were out of grace and on our way over the falls. I was more than happy to accept that grace, the safety line from the bank that would keep me from facing a long fall.

But that was all it was. Don't take me wrong, it was a big thing, this salvation, but it was a safety line. Rather, it was a

Beyond the Pale

series of safety lines offered to the world as a means to keep "the world" from eternal separation. Do you hear me? It was good, sweet even, but very impersonal. Jesus saved me, but as part of "the world".

My personal awakening, the real beginning of my relationship with Jesus began on that trip to Fiji. I was preparing for a bible study in which we were going to take part in communion, when quietly and simply I had a revelation. Jesus, who died on the cross for the world, would have died on the cross if Jeff Herring had been the sum total population of this tiny blue speck. I was sitting on the porch of a shack, in the middle of a pineapple plantation on Viti Levu, and I lost it! It was a sweaty-faced, snotty chin, heaving chest, hard to breath epiphany of my Creator's love for ME. He was offering me the chance to have a personal relationship with Him. Not just "the world". "Me."

I think the same sort of theory vs. practice, or faith vs. works, thing is part and parcel of this whole honoring everyone. Theory can accurately present solutions to problems, and faith is all that is required of us, but without the practice, or the works, we are diminishing the effectiveness and reason for both. Theory without practice or faith without works isn't invalid. They're just foolish.

The process is a reinforcing cycle, as well. It seems to become easier to honor others as you grow in relationship with them. Offense becomes more difficult the more "known" you

R.E.S.P.E.C.T.

are to each other. Where there was little common ground to find purchase on initially, relationship begets reciprocity. As the pale comes down, or as you began to step past it, things that were so strange become less and less so. For me, this doesn't just apply to those who are far outside my pale.

This would be super simple if I were just commanded to Love the brotherhood...they're pretty much all in my pale, aren't they? What about those Baptists? Or the Lutherans on the corner? How do you deal with those nutty Pentecostals? Remember, the command says "every person". How much of your bias against the brotherhood is because of ignorance? Have you given due consideration to the brotherhood, let alone loved them? I struggle enough with building little tiny forts inside my Judeao-Christian ethic fortress, before I even consider those outside of it.

In her 1951 collection of poems entitled *Oregon Mist*, Frances Holmstrom presents a certain poem that I think fits right here, really well. Frances is my great-grandmother, and happening upon this poem seemed serendipitous. I guess this quest has been in my blood for longer than I at first knew...

DENOMINATIONS
Oh, not for me are book and bell,
    Or rite, or doctrine deep, or creed,
But I will love my brother well,
    And prove my love in word and deed.

Beyond the Pale

> I step across the stony line
> > Between the priest and Pentecost.
> The truth within them both is mine,
> > And lesser things are better lost.

> It matters not what group we share,
> > Or what four walls we worship in.
> Our God is here, our God is there,
> > And all his own are blood and kin.

> These walls, that loom to us so high,
> > He sees not, looking from above,
> There are, to his all-seeing eye,
> > No fences on his fields of love.

I fall back to my earlier question. Does every person include Muslims? Atheists? Wiccan? Hindi? As Christians we may be the majority in the US, but we are only thirty percent of the world. How can we expect those who are "other" to come into relationship with our savior if we represent him so poorly? (Notice the "we" again?) I rephrase: How can I expect to be someone who models Christ to my neighbor when I can't even get along with my family?

I guess that the point I keep getting redirected to here is that, in order to honor everyone, I must be a person of varied

R.E.S.P.E.C.T.

relationships. If honor implies knowledge of, and knowledge of implies relationship, then more than a general honoring of humanity necessitates relationship with those who are different than I am.

The Pale: We are called to honor everyone.
The Truth: We are called to honor each one.

Beyond the Pale

CHAPTER 10 - PRACTICALLY RELATED

So how does this whole thing work? How do I grow in relationship with those outside my pale, or how do I begin to get rid of the pales in my life? Where do I buy the privilege-revealing goggles that will show me where I am taking part in the reducing of others for my own gain? How do I get to know the Jesus who came from outside of humanity's pale in order to save them each, individually, from the festering, stagnating environment each pale contains?

The take home lesson in this for me is that I must find a place that allows for me to grow in relationship with others. Our happy, creative God has given each of us the ability to critically take account of our own bias and blind-spots, and to use his brief, yet intense earthly modeling of how to "make it work" for ourselves. The model is simple, yet is made to fit virtually every gift, talent, passion, or lack thereof!

Here's what has worked for me:

1. Find a group of believers who will sharpen you, as iron sharpens iron, to grow in your relationship with each other and Dad. He chose twelve. Right now, my core group is about the same. These are people who I can trust with my shortcomings, my worst attributes and least likable disabilities. I know they

will hold me accountable, using God's Word as the rule, but will do so knowing that I will do the same for them.

2. Hang out with "others", trying to meet physical needs where possible, but growing in relationship no matter the "program". This is often the place that I've derailed. When this component of the model is neglected, then the club mentality ensues, constructing pales instead of breaking through them.

This has been the model I've tried to follow throughout my journey with Jesus. It doesn't ever work perfectly, but it always works. Dependent upon the group, the function has remained the same, though the process is often very divergent. Humanity is so varied that reaching out to those different than yourself will have a potentially infinite structural design. It's awesome!

When planning out this part of my sharing, I was torn between the decision of giving out examples of others who are doing an amazing job, in my estimation, of using their personalities, abilities, and opportunities to walk in Jesus' footsteps, and leaving it open-ended so as to not pigeonhole the possibilities. My wrestling match was short-lived, though, as some of these pale-busting, relationship-growing processes were just too cool to not share.

Night Strike - Bridgetown Inc. - Portland, Oregon

Practically Related

My brother lives near Portland, Oregon, and one community outreach group he pointed out to me that blows my mind is called Bridgetown Inc. They sponsor and organize a variety of community outreaches for a variety of people groups, but one of their activities really caught my attention. This event, called Night Strike, is one where volunteers gather under the Burnside Bridge and spend time with the people who are there. Many of the folks that get served by these volunteers are homeless, and over the past eight years these events have become a draw for the homeless community in Portland. Why do they do it? This is what their website says:

"Night Strike is a unique opportunity for people to gather under the Burnside Bridge on the park side of Naito Parkway every Thursday night and love people because people matter. It's an opportunity for members of Portland's homeless community to hang out, enjoy a hot meal, receive a free hair cut, shave, have their feet washed and have their old shoes/clothes/sleeping bags replaced. It is also a chance for you to come down and share in the experience, help serve the needs of the homeless in our community, and more importantly, invest in lives and build relationships with the people you meet."

That last line really caught my attention. Additionally, the site has an orientation video describing the outreach, and I was so excited to see and hear the focus on relationship building. No matter the role a volunteer finds themselves fulfilling, the goal is to grow in relationship with the served. Wash feet, but talk to the foot washee. Hand out sandwiches, but make sure to dialog with the recipient. Get to know someone who is outside of your pale as a means to remove it!

I am already planning a visit to the Burnside Bridge when I next visit my family in Portland . I can't wait to have a chance to observe and participate in a Night Strike, and do a little pale removal. It is incredible to think how simply this movement started with just a folding chair, a basin of water, and, as the executive administrator Marshall Snider states, "a desire to do something great". Honor everyone.
http://bridgetowninc.org/

Eastlake Community Church - Bothell, Washington

A few years ago, this church in Bothell, Washington got a bit of flack for a fundraiser they put on called "Drinks for Drinks". Oh, yes, they were serving beer at a church function. I had to look into this, as my Pentecostal roots were initially banging the warning tambourine. Sure enough, Christians and Beer in the same location. But that's not all, my friends. That was not the sum of the gathering…

The church raised a quarter of a million dollars during this campaign for a non-profit that provides clean drinking water to people in developing countries. $251,869 dollars as a means to honor everyone. I was blown away, again. As I checked out their website, I became more and more excited.

Practically Related

The group's homepage is my dream of what the church could be. This little bit should explain:
"EastLake is a non-denominational, inter-generational, multi-locational (is that a word?), somewhat disorganized church started by nine friends in 2005. For us, it's all about, all because of, and all for... Jesus. It's not about buildings with baristas, bowling alleys or bookstores. We want to embody the church Jesus had in mind and he never saw church as a *place* to go, but as a *people*... not a religious institution, but a movement of love and hope. We think this whole faith thing is at its best when it motivates selfless service, sacrifice, and love... caring about the things God cares about. As a family of faith, we are committed to **dispense hope** to our local communities and beyond... standing up for those who live on their knees by both *bringing* good news and *being* good news. We were all created to live for something larger than ourselves and God invites everyone, everywhere into this way of living."

Organism not organization. Messy, probably. A little less than perfect, as it is made up of people. Trying to grow in relationship with those who are "other"? Heaven, yes! The group's tag line is so awesome:

"Eastlake Bothell – Church for the Rest of Us"

I cannot wait to meet this part of my family, and hear a word from Ryan Meeks, the lead pastor of the gathering. You know the feeling when someone you love does something really cool? You want to jab the guy next to you and go,

"Hey, I'm related to that awesome person!" Yeah, that's how these cousins make me feel…
http://eastlakecc.com/bothell/

Youth With A Mission

In spite of the fact that it has been nearly twenty years since I was an active YWAMer, I can say, without a doubt, I would not have the relationship with God or others that I do now if I had not taken the YWAM challenge. This movement has been around for quite a while, and has an avenue for every imaginable personality, vision, or passion. What is YWAM, you ask? There were a few facetious monikers floating around in my day, and I'm sure they still are, such as Young Wolves After Maidens, or Young Women After Men, but the truth of the matter is this: Youth With a Mission is a group that creates environment for a pale reducing worldview. Their website explains it this way:

"Youth With A Mission is an international volunteer movement of Christians from many backgrounds, cultures and Christian traditions, dedicated to serving Jesus throughout the world. Also known as YWAM (pronounced "WHY-wham"), our purpose is simply to know God and to make Him known. When YWAM began in 1960, our main focus was giving young people opportunities to demonstrate the love of Jesus to the whole world, according to His command in Mark 16:15. Today, we still focus on youth, but we have members (known

as "YWAMers") of almost every age and many of our short-term efforts have grown into long-term endeavors that have impacted lives and nations.
YWAM has a decentralized structure that encourages new vision and the exploration of new ways to change lives through training, convey the message of the gospel and care for those in need. We are currently operating in more than 1000 locations in over 180 countries, with a staff of over 18,000."
http://ywam.org/

    I cannot encourage anyone strongly enough to find a way to involve themselves in a YWAM outreach. It changed my life. It will change yours, as well.

    Finally, and I don't mean this in the "old preacher" turn of phrase, I pray that what I've shared will persuade you to reflect on some of the pales you may have in your life. My beautiful and brilliant wife, while working with me on this little organization of my thoughts, opened the bible one night to a passage that she found relevant. For all of you single folks out there who are looking to get hitched, I recommend you "marry up". I did, and the benefits are legion. Anyway, her favorite passage of Dad's love letter is the following:
Isaiah 58:6-11
6-9"This is the kind of fast day I'm after:
 to break the chains of injustice,

get rid of exploitation in the workplace,
   free the oppressed,
   cancel debts.
What I'm interested in seeing you do is:
   sharing your food with the hungry,
   inviting the homeless poor into your homes,
   putting clothes on the shivering ill-clad,
   being available to your own families.
Do this and the lights will turn on,
   and your lives will turn around at once.
Your righteousness will pave your way.
   The God of glory will secure your passage.
Then when you pray, God will answer.
   You'll call out for help and I'll say, 'Here I am.'
9-12"If you get rid of unfair practices,
   quit blaming victims,
   quit gossiping about other people's sins,
If you are generous with the hungry
   and start giving yourselves to the down-and-out,
Your lives will begin to glow in the darkness,
   your shadowed lives will be bathed in sunlight.
I will always show you where to go.
   I'll give you a full life in the emptiest of places—
   firm muscles, strong bones.
You'll be like a well-watered garden,
   a gurgling spring that never runs dry.

You'll use the old rubble of past lives to build anew,
  rebuild the foundations from out of your past.
You'll be known as those who can fix anything,
  restore old ruins, rebuild and renovate,
  make the community livable again."

    I hope that I won't get in the way of being the person that God has planned. I hope that my search after doing the right thing will include being a person that can, with His help, fix anything. I want to glow! I don't want to be a hypocritical, judgmental, plank-eyed spiritual introvert who sacrifices real relationship on the altar of false, self-constructed safety. If everything that is belongs to Dad, why do I need a pale? If everyone I meet is an avatar of my creator, why would I push them away? If the model I endeavor to follow is one of a savior coming into my pale, sacrificing everything to do so, why would I do any differently?

    I end with a benediction, reader. My prayer is that you may see the face of God shining from and reflected in each one you meet.

Numbers 6: 24-26:
GOD bless you and keep you,
GOD smile on you and gift you,
GOD look you full in the face and make you prosper.

Beyond the Pale

Works Cited

Bunyan, John, Robert Lawson, and Lucy Aikin. *Pilgrim's Progress*. Philadelphia, PA: J.B. Lippincott, 1939. Print.

Fillon, Mike, "The Real Face Of Jesus: Advances in forensic science reveal the most famous face in history." *Popular Mechanics*. 7 Dec. 2002. Web. 20 July 2012.

http://www.popularmechanics.com/science/health/forensics/1282186

Holmstrom, Frances. *Oregon Mist*.Portland, OR: binfords & Mort Publishers, 1951. Print.

The Holy Bible: Containing the Old and New Testaments, Translated out of the Original Tongues and with the Former Translations Diligently Compared and Revised ; Commonly Known as the Authorized (King James) Version. Philadelphia: National Pub., 1978. Print.

MacIntosh, Peggy. "White privilege: unpacking the invisible knapsack" *Peace and Freedom* (July/August 1989): 10-12.

Tomblin, David, and Incorporated Television Company, prods. "The Prisoner." *The Prisoner*. ITC. 1967. Television.

www.ingramcontent.com/pod-product-compliance
Lightning Source LLC
LaVergne TN
LVHW051155080426
835508LV00021B/2633